CALCUTTA, CROW
and other fragments

Calcutta, Crow
and other fragments

Brinda Bose

HAWAKAL

hawakal

Published by Hawakal Publishers
185 Kali Temple Road, Nimta, Kolkata 700049
India

Email info@hawakal.com
Website www.hawakal.com

First edition July 2020

Cover concept and design: Romik Bose Mitra

ISBN: 978-81-945273-6-7

Price: 200 INR | 9.99 USD

Introduction

When my father died in 2016, it was as if I began to experience anew the city of my growing up. His passing coalesced all losses I had ever encountered in Calcutta into one loss— and crystallized so many lustrous memories of my city into one single, giant, glinting jewel. The days that followed glistened with words. I tried to write some of them down even as they disappeared, struggled, failed. These fragments were written in an insomniac rush over a few weeks then, and abandoned.

My mother passed away last month; Hawakal happened to write to me the same week asking if I had any words at all to share with them—to be turned, as if by magic, into this book—and the coincidence seemed both surreal and serendipitous. How does one fashion the transitory into sentences that stay? One doesn't. These fragments are a testament to that impossibility.

Calcutta, June 2020

CONTENTS

calcutta, crow I

anticipating turbulence
an old man heads stonily to the lavatory
his need greater than the hour of turbulent
skies

where is the storm in that calm night
what horrors lurk
what a cursed city
that a homecoming
is jarred by the shock of uncertain landing
the promise of home darkling and
sparkling
in a sepulchred sky
lurches into a jewelled breast flashing
glinting luring mocking
any city every city in arrival mode

inmycity
the air hangs low wet warm
sweaty streetdogs yelp and frisk and snap

baring rabied fangs, laggardly
at a lone girl
trotting homeward swaddled in anxious
bravado
a city ashen, turbulent,
sparking caution and caveats of
impoverished life
dyingcity livingcity survivingcity
pirouetting between despair rejection
devotion ennui
and passion

citylights like gems flung upward into a
sulky night

calcutta, crow II

what conversations do you hold with the
room you grew up in?
are they the colour texture stink of
seaweed
soaked in the spirit of briny seas
oliveblack with the dark weariness of
faraway lands
alive with the hope of survival in return
exquisitely hardy in refuge

remnants
most intimate and most distant
more difficult than fleeting friends and
lovers lost and found

that old room swam you through every fall
and nick
every ephemeral passing elation
swept out bloodcrusted bandages when
wounds healed
and smirked at your flickering jubilations

having no memory and all memory
no eyes and ears and nose and mouth and
fingers
but all eyes ears mouth nose fingers
your room braillemaps you each time you
return
tracking bruises that broke and made you

fingering lightly
all the laughter that birthed the crowsfeet
at the corners of your eyes

calcutta, crow III

finally only one street defines this city
the coffin of skeletal tramlines
where collegial ghosts
rest

on violent flashbacks
on laughter coiled in cobwebs
on raging literature crouched in crumbled
pages
precarious, predatory
on shelves holding crusted pavements
and gross management tomes to ransom

there was a time when all of poetry was a
wild and endless epiphany

before recollections rolled
anger roiled and ardour spent

retreading bookstreet now where time is
liquid and burning

drowning infusions sugarblack
melting argument
smoking love

whoever knew
that such an ageless street as this
the ageing might reclaim
hunting still

for themselves, for others, for books, coffee,
grass, frenzy and rapture
restless poems that spiral up and down
those grimy stairs
vomiting fear and tenderness
fervent, insomniac

calcutta, crow IV

crawling this city's face, grey termite
munching through a crumbling shelf two
millimetres a year, or less. remembrances
of what we said and did not say, what we
did, slept, loved, lied, cried. but so much
that we said we would do but have not,
burning and yearning through alleys of
conversations real and imagined.
calcutta, crow.

about all you know and think you know,
about us together and apart walking along
unbidden local traintracks and riverine,
those glances which have met and held. of a
time before we came to be, that a city
existed in which we were born and played
and hungered and wept, and knew, and did
not know
calcutta's crow

resolute
resilient
fretfully watching that odd tender touch
drop from your careless hand
on my shoulder

it has been so long and not so long at all
that the city has held us, screaming and
silent. all our lives when our lives have just
begun. is it the old man bergson who
meanders with us unbearably light, henri
henri hold on tight we said. oh is he the
third who walks always beside us
shadowboxes through our piled up
yesterdays and wipes the snot of obnoxious
recollection on our sleeves as they brush
against each other and smirk.
calcutta, crow

agnosco veteris vestigia flammae
feel once more the scars of the old flame
but what is that flame how high does it sear
to leer up the skirt of varicose thighs
where did it come from when did the
match blaze and smear
a fingertip of jasmine attar to the dip
behind my ear which your hand reached
out and licked
with languor

calcutta's crow
somnolent

satyr-ical
perched on the edge of the parapet peering
into our eyes as we wander together and

apart
there and here
rapt lost hidden in the stench of stories we
have shared in separate lives just like
those old framed blackandwhite replicas of
our future selves having neither history
nor logic that hang askew in that studio
along the dank corridor
on the first floor where clocks stand frozen
and no one visits

except us.
calcutta, crow

insomnia | amnesia | sleep.: a game

if there was a way to conjure up a condition mimicking the amnesiac, there would be no insomniacs. and our sleep: full of extraordinary tumult, whirling us before the footlights, letting us write our own farces and romances and tragedies— and then moving us on instantly, in a forgetting.

we lose sleep; memories crowd our sleeplessness. if we could will a suspension of memory, if the years, months, weeks, days and hours before we slumber would mechanically, tirelessly, erase themselves on a magic writing pad with ticking time, we would sleep, and perchance, dream ardent dreams, sweat in nightmares, scream in thrall—all birthed fresh, unmarked and unstale. that might be a sleep worth sleeping.

if immediate memory played tricks on us and disappeared at sleeptime, transporting us to lost days in rain and sun, we would float in such a charmed slumber, smile at the foolishness of distant images, comforted by their farawayness.

but that is not the game we want to play. we wish that there should be no memories at all. and no peace, no tranquility of incense smoke, no stretch of lime and cream pastoral space either.

instead there should be kaleidoscopic colours dancing light swirling and clashing the clash of cymbals the violence of drums growling bass guitars the sexiness of the sax—and all the perfumes of mountains, seas and cities wafting in together, scents of blossoms and vilest stenches steaming and frothing like acids in a crucible. there should be beauty and evil, murder and passion, backbreaking sisyphus labour, carnivals, feasting, hunger and thirst, blood, urine, spit, semen, white and black and bright fluids segued together in the run-up to sleep.

but there should be no memory. all should be new: no people we know, want, fear or despise, no places we have ever been to and lived in. no buildings we have loved and left, or crouched and cringed in. there should just be glorious-wild-terrible colour, light, sound and smell, now moulding into shapes, now telling tales of monsters and goblins and fairies, now breaking and scattering and shattering.

in which sleep would then swing through their crevices, warps and wefts: weaving its own patterns, speeding from languorous to racy in the wealth of a minute. in which sleep would reinvent every moment, clutching at dreams and nightmares, but losing each of them as they crossed. in which sleep would discard remembrances, and throw them into a sea teeming with whirlpools that would never bring back memory bodies on their resurgent returning waves—but suck them under and make them disappear.

the felling of insomnia by a willful amnesia: a fancy, a fantasy. and our sleep then swelling with all the drama we crave—raw, crisp, fresh and unfettered.

loss

loss compels loss, it looks like.
a book, some classes, a campus
all the pens I ever possessed
a few meals, sleep
a dream or two, a touch or three
laughing eyes
love, disagreement, argument
tenderness
a fading morning chill
a father and a mother.
a month is forever
and no time at all.

november: water

there's something solitary about november
like dark smudges on still water

like waiting for a friend to return from the
river of summer
(or is it from some mountain fall)
not knowing that a prewinter bite has
swallowed him whole

he's left behind
in the chair that he would sink into
a hole
shaped like his laughing mouth

december: tree

bare life.
bear
life.
the plenty, the lone.
another year is done for, done in.

january: gravestone

someone walked over my grave at least twenty times today.

each time i knew i could name the footfall, it lifted a heel and toe in tandem and hovered in the air above just out of touch. the face that matched its step fell out of step. my breath which caught, fell again, a little shorter, a little fainter, more sorrowing.

not knowing, yet knowing sharper, like a knife through flesh, for that missed step.

february: pocket

what is this gentle foreboding, or is it a foreclosing; a sense of something dropped, left behind, fallen out when I was not looking.

were you hiding in my pocket then, keeping my hand warm as it bunched in the chill, unaware of your blood leaking heat into mine. and then suddenly you were gone, my fingers frosty in the darkening sun.

or were you crouching in the crumpled innards of my bag, my numb nails searing accidentally in fumbling for the car keys, burnt and recoiling, searching for the cold comfort of steel and surprised by the skin of you.

or the smell of you, seeping through an assortment of my scattered selves, pens, hairbrush, notebook, phone, migraine pills, tissues with grubby dogeared ends buffeted by the jetsam of my life. anchored by a couple of keys lost and found a few times every day in those folds of cotton and zippers you occupied. if briefly.

or the sound of you, ringing lightly in my ear
at an odd moment of afternoon when I tossed my
head for the comfort of earrings swinging against
my neck. a low sound it was, almost a memory of
a whisper unheard. and then you fell out silently
like a word unspoken and I flailed a cupped hand
under my ear, my palm curved to catch a shooting
star.

kiss of thought

a late april evening floats on a zephyr.
ominous.
the enchantment of dark thought
drops
impatiently
on a radiant forehead,
a kiss so fleeting that it spawns no memory.

the weekend is only half done. there is
mockery in the grim beauty of the night
sky.

red is the now black

invocation 1

sleep curls like a flaccid ring of hair
between thumb and forefinger
thirst prowls in waves of crushed bedlinen
love waits
stroking a wisp of hair on your cheek

a dream implodes like a fat gooseberry in
the mouth

invocation 2

the clean cusp of your elbow
flesh that leans shyly over your
petticoatstring
a gossamer vein on the inside of your wrist,
quixotic
an earring that dangles, phallic

i come bearing gifts
my adoration and my fret
my dour skin and mottled threat

i bring you
rainlashes that dance on your dusty cheek
whispered breath where your neck curves
my venomous craving like acid bursting in
your face

dark fear pooling in ovaries rolling down
thighs congealing on calves
streaming terror not beauty
the colour of rejection
is the colour of blood

red is the now black

invocation 3

passion is always both enraged and tender
       it's where the shadow falls that
slays or spares, that is all

words that bleed and fly 1

for avijit roy in bangladesh, february, 2015: requiem

what now, this living hour in the dead of night. what is it about you that raises the hair on our arms tonight as you die for the words you wrote, felt, slept, and spoke. a dhaka pavement bleeds and weeps but is there insurrection on all the pavements of the world, are they all rising and shrieking in this our seething messy unruly grief that is going nowhere

because sharp brave words have lost their way in the grey frantic flapping middle where death and surveillance and vigilantism snicker and stride and where you can start squirting blood in so many directions that you can learn, or forget, to count. all your life you piled words on words bearing aloft the freedom of thought and the land of the free and the brave gave you bright promising skies to trail your letters of fire across to a homeland that was to celebrate your thoughts on freedom in a carnival of books. should we not howl at the horror of this massacre of the word that came flying over mountains and lakes searching for roots in the land of rain and rising rivers. and if we have stomach for more than horror there is irony too, to be hacked good and proper you need to be felled with fair books, you must be knived carrying the burden of the printed word, the spoken word, the heard word and the read word on your breathing walking talking person and it must be etched on your body with the dull pleasurable ache that brands your arms when you limp out of the fair of books that you travelled so far home to sell and buy: words. your words and their words and everybody's words but then suddenly in a bizarre coldblooded calm your words turn deathly pale and ghastly red and begin to spread and leak

until every book on every pavement from dhaka to all the cities of the known world is doused with the blood of the words they bear and the flesh that carries them, limping and triumphant, incarnadine

words that bleed and fly 2 .

for taslima nasreen in america, june 2015: aubade

and what now, when words rise like yeast and carry you over hoary oceans to a land that is yours and everybody else's or so they like to sing, but is not really yours in blood and tongue and glistening silverscaled fish and monsoon floods except in hyphenation. that land is warm with welcome, yes, with the laughter of sisterhood camaraderie solidarity support and the deep grinding sorrow of a brother's passing but it is not your land.

so you may land there but you shall not forget the words you left behind you in the lands you call your own, many cities that you had to leave one by one dhaka calcutta delhi trailing garlands of poems and prose and loves and conversations and writing, always writing. where can you go, where must you go, light and heavy on wings of words sharing stories and wine and the nostalgia of white. white summer sarees left behind at home... but wait, was that home? that adopted city of a tongue once-removed while you hungered and fought for a place in the grimy bangla sun on either side of two-nation borders. but then who cares about borders when lands on both sides grow hostile slouching into a dull sepia with memory searching for bold angry markings on the ground beneath lowering skies. there are now only shadows casting grim tales of émigré despair and hope and lives old and new are rolled up and hurled at the barbed wire fencing to pierce holes and squeeze dreams that are dead and dying through them like camels through eyes of needles

and some stories surf up on the other turf and plant words in a soil unknown yet intimate for the words are shared if the tongue rolls them differently and spits them out in shapes and sounds at once alien and one's own but just as you begin to believe that the roots are taking hold you must pack up your sarees and your stories in a weary suitcase and fly away again. into hiding they say but where will you hide how can you hide why should and would you hide when the words find you again and again and tear into you and out of you and speed away to slam into other faces and names and tongues. to beat and flay and form fresh flags

of words, just like all your white summer sarees waiting to be worn and crushed and soiled with passion and poetry, splendidly done and undone in beauty, sadness and rage

reprise

you said my eyes were like cactus flowers
springing like twin electric shocks
from thorns and frowns
you said you'd wade into my cactus flower
eyes
slain again and again by pleasure and
surprise

that was a poem I wrote in youth.

there were no flowers that were my eyes.
there was no you.
there were only wanton pauper-poems
careening about
till
the pennies ran out

spring and summer

a demented sun kissed her ritual spots.
shadows deepened on her furrowing face.
the dusty day clogged and crept, her drear
cloaked in fine facepowder

(freedom from her is a change of place)

Old bruises drift on a swell of tedium.
afternoons melt into lukewarm coffee.
her skin like paper creases in a hideous
grimace, like a gnome leering at a
retreating lover

(freedom from her is a change of face)

routine goes rancid, and crusty, and vile;
somersaults, and chokes on its bile. the
quotidian corrodes like a north indian
summer: she slashes and burns, turning
wonder to ashes

(freedom from her is a change of pace)

rain-parcel

you said I sat in a cane armchair on your verandah all night, reading. it was an armchair that no longer sits on the verandah in your house, the one you grew up in. it was the old armchair's ghost that I sat in and I was far, far from the house you grew up in, lying in a sleepless bed not reading not dreaming. inert. thinking of the house I grew up in and the road that runs all night under my window with trucks that rattle rudely all night every night rumbling through my bedclothes birthing lullabies carrying me toward restless slumber, ever carrying. but where I lie now in stoic noiselessness neither sleep nor dream is forthcoming, I take the train to the house you grew up in, I left mine just yesterday and now days and nights are wrapped in work and logic and nightmares of longing and belonging. and the rain that marches like a relentless army pounding on the roof and windows of the house you grew up in is the rain that sneaks into the crevices of the house I grew up in and mingles in story and song and rage and sorrow and seeps through its walls and floods its floors which turn into seas with patterns of mosaic that we wake up to at electric grey dawns. but here there is no rain only the trickery of sodden skies hidden in muddy clouds. promise that you will pack up a legion of rain from the armies drumming on your verandah that killed and buried the armchair that once sat there and promise that you will put it on a train to here with the suitcase fastened tight so that it cannot escape from those large windows with horizontal rails barring faces and hands of the peering sky from getting in. for if they got in such fusillades of rain would travel from the houses we grew up in to the barrenness of now and where would barrenness go in such a despair of homelessness? until we sort all that out and the rain is packed and sealed and dispatched, let me sit on the verandah in the house you grew up in and read in the armchair that once was.

fire showers

the fecund forests of uttarakhand
burning
the shocked thighs of jisha
burning
the crawling hunger of student strikers
burning
the shelled skin of droughtlands
burning
the daily perils of garment workers
burning
the ghastly guilt of farmer suicides
burning
the rampage of saffron
burning
the ferment of blue
burning
burning

how can there be rain?

desolation

it takes death to teach us
that dying is not desolation,
living is.
for that we have death to thank,
for desolation
is
all.

window

so much beauty in crevices of grey
steely promise
in bar and grill, star and flower.

so much menace
in a window shut wide open
sheeted with darkness.

poetry. still.

your door deepens with a silhouette.
your door empties

a boat
lies disconsolate on the river today
damp with yesterday's fog.

dinner burns slightly acrid.
you both eat it, for bitter-coloured
intestines

wrapped in brownpaper thoughts
the morning news is cold, ablaze.

only a snatch of voice bears you aloft
to a place you want to be, fading

blood, skin, stone and bone batter
homes and hills, roads and trees, rivers and
seas.

cries and whispers
gutted in a red room. the colour spills out
of the door and runs like a river down the
road outside your home into the
neighbour's house like the juice of a
crushed pomegranate cruising down a chin

poetry. still.

9 788194 527367